ICE SKATING

THE INCREDIBLE MICHELLE KWAN

by Michael Sandler

Consultant: Kenny Moir
Executive Director of Figure Skating
Chelsea Piers
New York, NY

BEARPORT
PUBLISHING

New York, New York

Credits

Cover and title page, ©AP Photo/Paul Chiasson; 4, © STEPHEN JAFFE/AFP/Getty Images; 5, © CARLO ALLEGRI/AFP/Getty Images; 6, © Robert Laberge/Getty Images; 7, © YURI KADOBNOV/AFP/Getty Images; 8, © Sports Illustrated/Robert Beck; 9, © Neal Preston/CORBIS; 10, © AP Photo/John Redman; 11, © Isabel Snyder/CORBIS OUTLINE; 12, © Bryan Allen; 13, © Neal Preston/CORBIS; 14, © Neal Preston/CORBIS; 15, © SAN BERNADINO SUN/GABRIEL ACOSTA/CORBIS SYGMA; 16, © J. Barry Mittan; 17, © REUTERS/Fred Prouser; 18, © Todd Warshaw/ALLSPORT/Getty Images; 19, © CARLO ALLEGRI/AFP/Getty Images; 20, © American Broadcasting Companies, Inc.; 21, © AP Photo/Cliff Schiappa; 22, © AP Photo/Damian Dovarganes; 23, © AP Photo/Beth A. Keiser; 24, © Sports Illustrated/Bob Martin; 25, © Doug Pensinger/ Getty Images; 26, © Andrew Gombert/Sports Illustrated; 27, © AP Photo/Amy Sancetta.

Publisher: Kenn Goin
Project Editor: Lisa Wiseman
Creative Director: Spencer Brinker
Original Design: Ralph Cosentino

Library of Congress Cataloging-in-Publication Data

Sandler, Michael.
  Ice skating : the incredible Michelle Kwan / by Michael Sandler.
      p. cm. — (Upsets & comebacks)
  Includes bibliographical references and index.
  ISBN-13: 978-1-59716-252-4 (library binding)
  ISBN-10: 1-59716-252-3 (library binding)
  ISBN-13: 978-1-59716-280-7 (pbk.)
  ISBN-10: 1-59716-280-9 (pbk.)
  1. Kwan, Michelle, 1980—Juvenile literature. 2. Figure skaters—United States—
Biography—Juvenile literature. 3. Women figure skaters—United States—Biography—
Juvenile literature. I. Title. II. Series.

  GV850.K93S36 2007
  796.91'2—dc22

                              2006010792

For more information, write to Bearport Publishing Company, Inc., 101 Fifth Avenue, Suite 6R, New York, New York 10003. Printed in the United States of America.

10 9 8 7 6 5 4 3 2 1

Table of Contents

Moment of Truth

It was the night before the 1998 U.S. Nationals. Michelle Kwan couldn't sleep. She tossed and turned in her bed for hours.

The next morning, Michelle had to put her worries aside. It was time to skate. This event was her chance to come back from a terrible year.

The gold-medal winner at the U.S. Nationals gets the chance to skate at the Winter Olympics.

Michelle on the ice at the 1998 Nationals

Once, Michelle had been a champion. Her grace and skill had amazed judges and fans. Then everything went wrong. Her **confidence** faded. She wasn't winning as many competitions. She lost her joy for the sport.

Many young skaters had risen to the top and then quickly disappeared. As she glided onto the ice, people wondered if this was the end for Michelle.

During better times, Michelle Kwan performs at the World Championships in 1996.

Figure Skating

Figure skating can be a nerve-racking sport. Scores between **competitors** can be separated by only a fraction of a point.

In competitions, skaters perform a long and a short program in front of judges. During both programs, skaters show off their **technical** and **artistic** skills. In the short program, each skater performs a fixed set of moves. They are judged on how well they do compared to the others. In the long program, skaters create routines matched to music and their own talents.

Shizuka Arakawa, of Japan, in mid-jump during her short program at the 2006 Winter Olympics

As each skater performs combinations of jumps, turns, and spins, judges watch and award points. One wrong move can mean the difference between winning and losing.

Sasha Cohen

Sasha Cohen and Irina Slutskaya were favorites at the 2006 Winter Olympics. When both fell during their long programs, Shizuka Arakawa took the gold medal.

Learning to Fall

When Michelle was only five years old, she begged her parents to let her ice skate. At first, they said that she was too young. However, Michelle kept asking. Finally, they gave in and let Michelle and her older sister, Karen, give it a try.

Michelle poses for a photo with her father, Danny; her mother, Estella; and her brother, Ron, in 1997.

Michelle took to the ice at once. One of the first things she learned was how to fall without hurting herself. Instructors don't want young skaters to get **injured**. She was also taught how to **stroke** and glide and turn and jump.

Michelle was always in a hurry. "Teach me more," she urged.

Michelle gets some help after a fall.

Michelle and Karen grew up in Torrance, California, a city near Los Angeles.

A Dream Is Born

Even when Michelle wasn't skating, she was thinking and dreaming about the sport. By age seven, Michelle had a goal—to win gold medals. She'd watched skater Brian Boitano on television as he won the top medal at the Calgary Winter Olympics. Michelle wanted to spiral through the air and to compete with the best, just like Brian.

Michelle's idol, American figure skater Brian Boitano

Michelle worked hard. By the time she was eight years old, she and Karen were training with a **professional** instructor. They woke up five days a week at 4:30 a.m. and headed to the rink.

Karen is two years older than Michelle.

At age seven, Michelle entered her first skating competition. She won first place.

Leaving Home

Michelle and Karen were entering contests and often winning. They kept moving up to higher levels of competition. To keep improving, however, they needed even more time on the ice.

When Michelle was 11 years old her parents made a decision. She and Karen would go to live at a skating **facility** called Ice Castle. There they could breathe ice skating seven days a week.

Ice Castle International Training Center, in Lake Arrowhead, California

Being away from home wasn't easy. Ice Castle was two hours away from Torrance. The sisters were rarely able to go home on the weekends.

Michelle, Karen, and their dad at Ice Castle

Danny Kwan made a four-hour round-trip drive each day to spend evenings with his daughters at Ice Castle.

Passing the Test

At Ice Castle, Michelle's coach, Frank Carroll, was teaching her a lot of new things. He showed her how to stay calm after making a mistake. He also taught her how to skate through a fall.

Michelle practicing with her coach, Frank Carroll

Michelle was winning medals at the junior level. However, things weren't moving fast enough for her. She didn't just want to **compete** against young skaters. She wanted to skate against the best!

Frank thought Michelle should **progress** slowly. Michelle, though, felt differently. One day, when Frank wasn't around, she took the test to become a senior skater. Twelve-year-old Michelle passed with flying colors!

Michelle and Karen lacing up their skates

At first, Frank was mad when he found out that Michelle had taken the skating test. Later he laughed about it. Michelle was clearly ready for the next level.

A Rising Star

It didn't take Michelle long to prove that she could compete against the country's best skaters. At her first senior-level championship in 1993, she finished in sixth place, ahead of many older skaters.

Later that year, she took first place at another senior-level contest in Texas. Success was coming fast.

Michelle skating at the 1993 Olympic Festival in San Antonio, Texas, where she took first place

Then, at the U.S. Nationals in 1994, Michelle finished with the silver medal. The top two skaters were supposed to make the U.S. Olympic team. It seemed that Michelle had **qualified**.

In a surprise move, however, officials named skater Nancy Kerrigan to the team instead. Michelle was disappointed, but now everyone knew that she was a rising star!

Although Michelle didn't skate in the 1994 Winter Olympics in Norway, she traveled there as an alternate.

Though she skated at the adult level, Michelle was still very much a kid. In 1994, she dressed up as Fred Flintstone for Halloween.

Champion

Michelle broke into figure skating's **elite** in 1996. She was fearless. Michelle loved being on the ice, and the judges couldn't help but notice. At every competition, joy and confidence shone through in her performance.

Michelle performing a jump at the 1996 Nationals

Her spinning, swirling long program earned a first-place vote from every judge at the U.S. Nationals. Then it was on to the World Championships. As Michelle waited to skate, **defending champion** Lu Chen performed a **masterful** program with six triple jumps. When Michelle's turn arrived, she wanted to do even better. By adding an unplanned seventh triple to her own program, Michelle skated away with the gold.

Michelle skates from the podium after receiving the gold medal at the 1996 World Championships. Behind her is silver medalist Lu Chen.

 At age 16, Michelle was the youngest American world champion ever!

Falling Down

Michelle was flying high. "There was nowhere to go but up," she wrote. "There was nothing around me but sky."

Yet the very next year, Michelle fell back to Earth. Life at the top was hard and filled with **pressure**. Reporters demanded interviews. Competitors made Michelle their target. Everyone wanted to beat the champion. The joy Michelle felt as a skater began to disappear.

Michelle sits for an interview.

At the 1997 Nationals, Michelle fell twice. A younger skater, Tara Lipinski, skated away with the gold. At the World Championships that year, Michelle missed a jump and burst into tears. Again, Tara took first place. Was it already over for Michelle?

Michelle's loss at the 1997 Nationals was her first one in almost a year.

Michelle falls during her long program at the 1997 Nationals in Nashville, Tennessee.

Coming Back

As the 1998 Nationals drew near, things seemed to become even worse. A **stress fracture** kept Michelle from skating for two months. Then, while warming up for the Nationals, Michelle repeatedly missed her jumps.

Michelle had to wear a cast after she injured her foot.

After watching her mistakes during practice, the crowd waited nervously as Michelle got ready to perform. Were they watching the end of a promising young skater's career? The answer was clear as soon as Michelle started skating: No!

Michelle skated beautifully in both the short and long programs. She glided over the ice with elegance and grace. Some called it the "greatest performance ever by an American skater." Michelle easily won the gold.

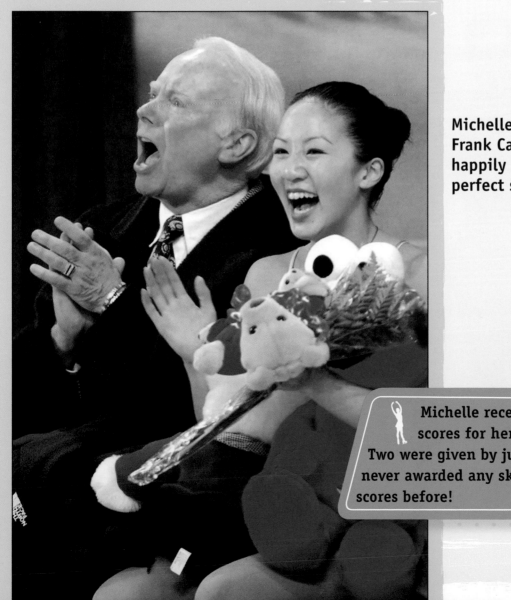

Michelle and her coach, Frank Carroll, react happily to Michelle's perfect scores.

Michelle received 15 perfect scores for her two programs. Two were given by judges who had never awarded any skater perfect scores before!

Michelle's victory marked the beginning of her comeback. It began a winning streak unlike any the skating world had ever seen before.

She won the U.S. Nationals seven years straight! She won four more World Championships. During Michelle's great run, no skater received more gold medals or gathered more perfect marks from judges.

Michelle, Tara Lipinski, and Lu Chen pose with their medals at the 1998 Winter Olympics.

Only one goal escaped her—winning Olympic gold. In 1998, Tara Lipinski beat her with a once-in-a-lifetime performance. So Michelle had to settle for a silver medal.

At the 2002 Olympics, Michelle left with a bronze. Other skaters might have quit after a second disappointment. Michelle, however, bounced right back to win the 2003 World Championships.

Michelle flies through the air at the 2003 World Championships.

Michelle has received a record 42 perfect marks in U.S. National competitions.

No Regrets

The 2006 Winter Games seemed like the last chance for Michelle to earn an Olympic gold. Sadly, it wouldn't happen. Suffering from an injury, Michelle **withdrew** even before the games began. Perhaps she could have skated, but she wouldn't have been at her best.

Her eyes filled with tears as she faced reporters with the news. Then she looked up and smiled. "I have no **regrets**," she said. "I tried my hardest, and if I don't win the gold, it's okay."

Michelle announcing her withdrawal from the 2006 Winter Olympics at a press conference

Few have tried harder. Few have battled back again and again to achieve as much success as the incredible Michelle Kwan.

Sonja Henie is the only woman skater who has won more World Championships than Michelle. This legendary Norwegian skater took ten straight titles from 1927 to 1936.

Just the Facts

More about Michelle Kwan and Figure Skating

★ **A Movie Star**—Michelle has appeared in two movies. She was the voice of an animated character in *Mulan 2* (2005), and she played herself in the film *Ice Princess* (2005).

★ **Good Luck Charm**—At every competition, Michelle wears a gold necklace with a dragon charm. The necklace is a gift from her grandmother. Michelle believes it gives her good luck.

★ **Sidelined**—Until an injury sidelined her for three weeks when she was 16 years old, Michelle had never spent 48 hours away from her skates.

Timeline

This timeline shows some important events in Michelle Kwan's career.

★ **1980**
Michelle is born in Torrance, California.

★ **1991**
Michelle and Karen begin living and training at Ice Castle.

★ **1992**
Michelle passes the senior skating test.

1980   **1985**   **1990**

★ **1993**
Michelle wins her first senior-level contest.

★ **Ancient Skates**—The oldest known ice skates date back to about 3000 B.C.! They were made with blades of animal bone and were probably used to cross frozen rivers and lakes.

★ **An Old Sport**—Figure skating is one of the oldest sports at the Winter Olympics. The first competition was at the 1908 London Olympics.

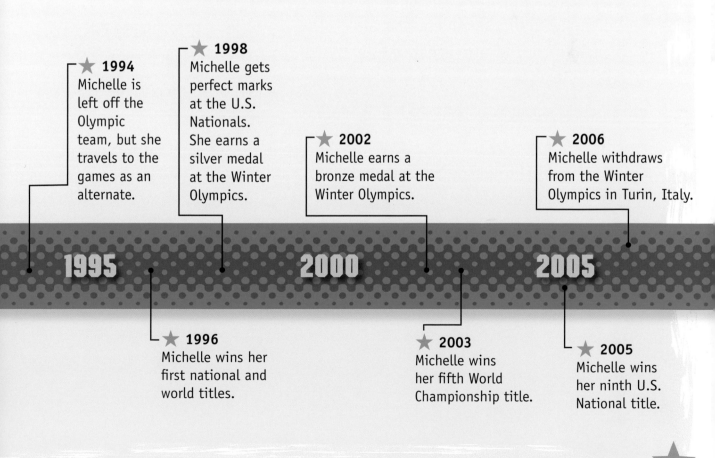

★ **1994** Michelle is left off the Olympic team, but she travels to the games as an alternate.

★ **1998** Michelle gets perfect marks at the U.S. Nationals. She earns a silver medal at the Winter Olympics.

★ **2002** Michelle earns a bronze medal at the Winter Olympics.

★ **2006** Michelle withdraws from the Winter Olympics in Turin, Italy.

1995

2000

2005

★ **1996** Michelle wins her first national and world titles.

★ **2003** Michelle wins her fifth World Championship title.

★ **2005** Michelle wins her ninth U.S. National title.

Glossary

artistic (ar-TIS-tik) having to do with a skater's ability to perform moves in an imaginative and creative way

compete (kuhm-PEET) to try as hard as possible in order to win

competitors (kuhm-PET-i-turz) people who take part in a contest or sporting event

confidence (KON-fuh-duhnss) when a person has a strong belief in his or her own ability

defending champion (di-FEN-ding CHAM-pee-uhn) the athlete who won an event the last time it was held

elite (i-LEET) people at the very top of their game

facility (fuh-SIL-uh-tee) a building or place where services are provided

injured (IN-jurd) hurt

masterful (MASS-tur-ful) powerful; very skilled

pressure (PRESH-ur) a heavy burden; strain

professional (pruh-FESH-uh-nuhl) getting paid to do something rather than just doing it for fun

progress (pruh-GRESS) to move forward

qualified (KWAHL-uh-fyed) earned entry into an event by performing well

regrets (ri-GRETS) to be sorry or sad about something

stress fracture (STRESS FRAK-chur) a partially broken bone

stroke (STROHK) to push off from the ice with one foot

technical (TEK-nuh-kuhl) having to do with a skater's ability to perform specific moves, including jumps and spins

withdrew (with-DROO) left; pulled out

Bibliography

Epstein, Edward Z. *Born to Skate: The Michelle Kwan Story.* New York: Ballantine (1997).

Kwan, Michelle, as told to Laura M. James. *Michelle Kwan: Heart of a Champion.* New York: Scholastic (1997).

The New York Times

Sports Illustrated

Read More

Jones, Jen. *Figure Skating for Fun!.* Minneapolis, MN: Compass Point Books (2006).

Kwan, Michelle. *Michelle Kwan: My Special Moments.* New York: Volo (2001).

Milton, Steve. *Figure Skating Champions.* Ontario, Canada: Firefly Books (2002).

Stewart, Mark. *Michelle Kwan: Quest for Gold.* Brookfield, CT: Millbrook Press (2002).

Learn More Online

Visit these Web sites to learn more about Michelle Kwan and the Winter Olympics:

www.infoplease.com/ipsa/A0115110.html

www.usfigureskating.org/AthleteBio.asp?id=2267

www.usoc.org/26_1145.htm

Index

About the Author

Michael Sandler lives and writes in Brooklyn, New York.
He has written numerous books on sports for children and
young adults.